# Our Love,
# Love & Morals

# Our Love,
# Love & Morals

Arelis Soto

**To order additional copies of this book, contact:**
Palibrio
1-877-407-5847
www.Palibrio.com
ordenes@palibrio.com
335184

# Contents

# Our Love

Asleep

you & I

you

awaken me

once again

wanting

our love &

always wanting

more & more

asleep, you

awaken me

we awaken, together &

fall asleep

once again

asleep you & I

our love

always

Arelis Soto

# I Never Meant To Hurt You

I never meant to

hurt you,

but there are times

that a little girl

grows, I was helpless

I never meant to hurt you,

but I had to get through

my own situation

I'm thankful for the guidance

and there you are standing

in front of me showing

me that you love me

I never meant to hurt you

* This poem is of transition to maturity

# To Hope Happily

Waiting

hoping happily

happiness

will endure

longingly

waiting

happiness

will endure

the waiting is

no longer

# Within My Heart

You are the sparkle that

remains within my heart

You are the love with me

whether near or far & if

by chance I forgot to

tell you that I love you,

well here's my love

today.

# Calm

She walks into her room
every night after dealing with all
the daily things
& there is her man
asleep waiting for her
with their favorite pillow
in his hands
she joins him in bed and
they share their breath
together, asleep in his calm
she wants to remain forever
always every night, there is her
man asleep waiting for her with
her with their breath together, asleep
in this calm she wants to remain forever
always every night, there is her man
asleep waiting for her with her with
their favorite pillow in his hands, she
joins him in bed they share their
breath together.

Arelis Soto

# His Hands

His hands are lumpy & soft
warm & sweetly moist gentle
& tender he is best without
a word said, gentle and tender
he is best without a word
his hands are lumpy and soft
warm and sweetly moist gentle &
tender

# Hidden

After you have
hidden me, there
won't be
anything to hide
& we will only
love each other
uniquely

# Still Breathing

Message at the front desk from you
Message at the front desk a card from you
Message at the front desk & a gift from you
Message at the front desk & your card says,


"I Love You"


Message at the front desk, I'm still
breathing & I'm missing you
Message at the front desk &, I'm still
breathing, missing you,& I love you too.

# Loyalty

When I say I see only
loyalty
I say it is only
loyalty I see

# *Raveled*

He gets raveled up
in anger if he don't get his
kissing, hugging & loving always
talking & worrying, fretting with
me about getting my loving for him
tossing & turning if he isn't close
to me, Co-Co love heartbeat, he angers
up furiously, he says "alright!", but he
isn't "alright!", Co-Co love heartbeat, he angers
furiously, he says "alright!", when we are togetherly loyally
togetherly man mine &
is more than "alright!", when close to me, but he gets
raveled up, in anger, if he
don't get his kissing hugging &
loving always getting my loving for
only him, man mine

# Silver & Platinum

Do I receive plenty of
Silver and platinum jewelry?
Yes, I receive all kinds of jewelry.
all kinds and forms of jewelry
trinkets, I am grateful and
happy with my gifts.
Are they from a secret admirer?
Yes, one secret admirer. Thank you.

* Transition of receiving and responding.
  Serenative, commencing stage of dating.
  A probability.

Arelis Soto

# It Isn't A Question

It isn't

a question

for what?

It's meant to be

shall be

It isn't

a question

# Time Passes

Time passes

by

&

summer

surpasses

stress

the fall

enters

time passes

by

again

September

starts

&

fall

enters

# For Keeps

For keeps, when I receive your
heart for keeps your heart
that you've relinquished
to me I shall keep,& though
in your emotional despair
you assumed that you & I
would never be, now in reality
you have relinquished your heart
to me & therefore I shall keep
it safely as I do my own, two hearts
become one!

# Sitting At The Table

She sits on top of a folded cloth
with a cup of tea at the table
she stares at the walls & she
awaits, he enters the room
they stare at each other,
she sits on top of a folded
clothe with a cup of tea
at the table, they sit together
at the table
they drink together

Arelis Soto

# Time For Fun

Time for fun

&

we

enjoy

our days

time for fun

in our own special

ways, time for fun

& we enjoy our days

by ourselves

or with friends

# El Escuchar

When listening
if something goes wrong
choose us, all the time
warning & choose us
a familiar tradition
when listening . . . etc,
if something goes wrong
choose us all the time
warning & choose us
a familiar tradition

# Whisper Lovingly

He tells me lovingly

&

I say in return

whispering

"Because you give me the fire of your love to keep

&

take mine, the fire of my love & heart

to keep & yes, I am your exact age

"A safe & warm orangey fire that we have becomed",

he tells me loving lovingly

He tells me lovingly

&

I say in return

whispering

take my love & heart to keep

&

He tells me lovingly

# Traveling

No-matter
where I am
walking around
traveling
doing
my own thing
outside
safety is
always
with me
No-matter where I am
walking around
or traveling
doing own my thing
outside safety is
always with me

# April & May

In my new month of
April & of May to you
Dear I say, a new life
is dawning & joy
continues in my new
month of April & of May
together us, two in love
forever in my new month
of April & of May to you
Dear I say
&
joy
continues

# Hides The European

The uniqueness radiates, so
indigenous the color it hides
the European part of the female
the pride that demonstrates
uniqueness
the uniqueness is such rarity, it also
flows with big locks & smoothly
uniqueness
the uniqueness
radiates, so indigenous my color
hides the European part of the female
the pride that demonstrates
my uniqueness in rarity
for the pride of all of thee
proudly, but humbly
for the pride of all of thee
It hides all of thee proudly,
but humbly
for the pride of all of thee

# The Broad Sea

When I spread my wings to soar
above the broad sea
I see my companion is right there
with me
other birds fly by & there
he is my beloved still there with me
lively & vividly completely
The sky is so clear when I spread
my wings to soar, above the broad sea
We meet at our selective mountainside
when we spread our wings to soar
above the broad sea
The sky is clear

# Heat Sting

Heat sting

under the sun

dangerous

get sunblock

the broken ozone layer

dangerous

get sunblock

follow instructions

warning

heat sting

broken ozone layer

warning

remember

get sunblock

# Self-Love-2003

Self-love

solitude

all forms

self-love

accompanied

self-love

from solitude

to being

accompanied

&

it starts with

"Hello"

& we depart & go

into our solitude

or socializing

once more either in solace

or accompanied or in our

solace

self-love

# To His Pleasure

To his pleasure
My one face true
stares at me constant in
his ways runs his fingers
through my brunette trestles,
longer to his pleasure
& healthy he remains
He my one face true love
stares at me & wins
my gaze constantly,
I his old, but new love
my one face true

Arelis Soto

# Pink Drinks

Pink drinks to drink dunkin'

&

I still watch the racing tracking

around me

Pink drinks to drink

# Wait

Wait a China moon
tingling laugh
moon look northern plants
elsewhere the cloud

# Haiku #6

Boom boom ba boom boom
I walked the happy pathway
Boom boom ba boom boom

# I Miss You

I miss you for you love me
I miss you
for your mine & I am yours
I miss you for you love me
eternally even if you are
near for you are mine &
I am yours for you love me
& I love you

# *Haiku #3*

Concurrently congruent

love actually

Concurrently congruent

And So

When I say there is love

with me & you

you & me

it is because

I only accept loyalty

when I say there only love

with me & you

you & me

it is because love exists

it is because

I only accept loyalty

& so

our love

will

literally

have its

history

we will be

loyally

lovingly

it is because love exists

& so

our love exists

with me & you

you & me

& so

& so

our love

exists

# All A Love Of Mine

My only love all a love

of mine truly & really

you are

heartfelty

together

my only love

all a love of

mine all for me

you are

we are

heartfeltly

together

my only love

truly & really

# Haiku #2

Wet natural rock into the
day's sunlight
Wet natural rock.

*3/20/06.

# Pink Summersweet

Pink summersweet is when we are too
irresistible for one another
& Pink inpatients
emerge, could be possibly purplish,
no burns at all just metaphoric & illustrative
between you & I,
a Pink summersweet
is too irresistible for us, between you & I, we are, just for
one another metaphoric, Pink Impatiens
emerge, could be possibly dark purplish,
with no burns, for the warmth spoken are warmth
that describe the warmth
that emerges between you & I
our, Pink Impatiens in Pink Summersweet
the sun afire all ablaze, or in winter glow,
foam flower that help describe the warmth
that we give to each other
when you surround me and I surround you
winterglow foam, Pink Summersweet & all
other seasons in between

# *Pink Lavender*

Pink lavender love on square

Pink lavender

huge big

Pink lavender diamonds

round

&

round

small,

petite

Pink lavender

# Our Love & Morals

Morals

love

Morals

Our

Love

Morals

our

own

love

# Solar

Algovariable
follows the Algostar
the night is mine
and all the stars, the Solar Orbit
natural all the worldwide stars
Our Spawn of Stars, I am the night,
the Solar Orbit, Algovariable, Algostar
Solar System, the night is mine, I am
the night, eclipse, electric, our spawn
of stars, generated, the night is mine,&
the stars rebussed, in their republic, rescinded,
eclipsed, the night is mine the immaculate wind all of it
& within I am the night, The Solar Orbit
all of the worldwide stars are mine
Algovariable, follows the Algostar, the
Solar Orbit natural

# All

All of you, all of me
just me, just you
all of me & all of you
lovingly
all pleasing
all of you, all of me
is just you & just me
8:00 pm . . .

# Midnight Blue

Among the midnight sky, we look above,
my love and there is nothing that can
be taken away from me & you. For
everyone has the right to enjoy
any color, natural around their own.
You have given me that right. And
I have given it to you in return. There
is nothing that can be taken away from
me & you; it's just me & you it's us two,
among the midnight blue sky, dressed
in black clothes & there is nothing
that is taken away from me & you,
safely "We Are One." & colors of clothes
may vary

# No Boundaries

The travel in the sky
back & forth
up and down
all around
no boundaries
they find their point
somehow, someway
they remain together
all around
they
find their
point, birds

# Height Of A Man

The height of a man
I have measured in your eyes
The tallness within you
I have seen
with soft and gentle eyes
the niceness you have for
me, the height of a man
I have measured in your eyes
when you speak to me
straight forwardly
or rhetorically
I have seen
The height of a man
the tallness within you
I have measured
In your eyes

# La Verdad Mi Amor

Y si me amas intensamente te comprendo, y si siempre quieres
estar a mi lado

te comprendo

y si siempre quieres estar a mi lado, te comprendo

y si me necesitas

siempre contigo y me proteges, te comprendo, y por eso me
preguntan

si te amo y le contesto a la gente, "Si lo amo."

Y si me amas intensamente te comprendo, y si

siempre quieres estar a mi lado, te comprendo, y si me cuidas

en todo publico te comprendo

y si me necesitas siempre, te comprendo, y por eso cuando me
preguntan si te amo

le contesto a la gente

# *Si lo amo*

y no es mentira, es la verdad, porque me amas con todas tus fuerzas,
y me amas

intensamente, te comprendo, y te amo

también, y aunque no conteste en un momento recuérdate, mi amor,
que te amo

Y si siempre quieres estar a mi lado

Si siempre me necesitas contigo

Recuérdate, mi amor, que te amo igualmente

Y si siempre me necesitas contigo

Recuérdate, mi amor, que te amo

Y si me cuidas en todo publico te comprendo

Por eso cuando

me preguntan, si te amo le contesto

a la gente, "Si lo amo",

Y no es mentira es la verdad Y aunque no conteste en un
momento recuérdate, mi amor

que te amo

*O*

Donde aye comprensión

ahí es donde vuelve el amor

ese que me ama sin parar y con mucha ternura

Comprensión pasión leal

Ahí es donde

vuelve el amor

pasión ferviente

leal

ahí es donde esta

o

vuelve el amor

# Solos

La arena abrigarte

mirada entre

tu y yo

hablamos

cosas fieles

amorosos

la noche

oscura

nos llenamos

de besos

y todo

amoroso

hablamos

entre

tu y yo

nosotros

solos

nuestras

miradas

están puestas

entre tú y yo

mirándonos

nuestras bocas se silencian

con nuestros besos entre tu y yo

cada paso dice algo

fiel, nuestras bocas se silencian bocas fieles amorosas la noche

oscura nos llenamos de besos y todo amorosos hablamos

entre tú y yo con nuestros besos nosotros solos fieles

con bocas amorosas

vivos, nuestra locura sana hablamos son nuestras bocas fieles de
silencio

Solos

bocas fieles amorosas,

enamoradas

nuestras bocas se silencian

La arena abrigarte

estamos solos

enamorados

# Nunca

Donde quiera que me digas

que

me quieres

recuérdate que aun el

viento te dice

que

te quiero igualmente

Oye, donde quiera que me digas que me quieras recuérdate que
el

viento te dice que te quiero igual

que te quiero igual

porque es fácil y el viento aun te dice que te quiero

y te trae

y regresas

pero nunca te vas

es tu canción es fácil y por eso

nunca fuiste

es fácil y por eso

nunca te vas

# Lo Mejor

Lo mejor

que me entregas

en amor

y nunca

suficiente

ni para ti ni para mí

porque

lo mejor

que me entregas

en amor

es lo mejor

y nunca es suficiente

ni para ti ni para mí

y es siempre

es suficiente

nos entendemos

# Tu Grito De Amor

Tu grito de amor

viene a mi corazón

y nos encontramos

oyes mi voz

va a tu corazón

los novios

que somos

como amigos que somos

Tu grito de amor viene a mi corazón y nos encontramos oyes mi voz

oigo tu voz en nuestro dos corazones que se hacen uno somos unidos

Tu corazón y mi corazón siempre nos encontramos

porque siempre estamos juntos algo bello

viene a mi corazón somos unidos nuestro dos corazones que se hacen uno

estamos juntos y te veo como algo bien bello

# Aun Tuya

El amor es apaciguar

tu tensión

aun tu ser

tuya

pero

tus tensiones

se apacigua

entre

nuestro

amor, el amor

es todo

lo que

dices, es verdad pero lo único

que apacigua tu tensión es aun tu

ser

todo mío y yo ser toda tuya

entre nuestro amor

# Reconozco

Entro en mi jardín

miro a mis Rosas

Tulipanes

y a mis otras flores y reconozco

con

regocijo

que

Estoy feliz con riqueza

miro a mis Rosas

Tulipanes

y

A mis otras flores

le hecho agua

Y

reconozco

que estoy feliz con riqueza

Arelis Soto

# No Boundaries

We

travel together

in the sky back & forth

up and down all around no boundaries

We find our

point

somehow, someway

we remain

together

all around

We find our

point

Purple Birds

# One True Felt Love

Two in love can make a difference

Two in love that are one

within each other can make a difference and truly love

one another

One true felt love

can make a difference

two in love

two that are one

and to truly love one another

A man & his woman

in completeness

# Notes & Letters
# A Love Letter of Many

Notes and letters between my beloved & me

love words

spoken


so many

between

my beloved and me

the most intense

message


was at first love glance

Humongous in love words spoken

beauty

between my beloved & me love words spoken

a love letter in silently

but the most intense message was at first love glance

humongous in love words spoken

Our love letter in silently

and therefore

most of all

Notes and letters between my beloved and me

Love words spoken so many words between my beloved and
me

Arelis Soto

## Rubies

When I wear
his rubies it will be because
I am only his

The rubies I wear
will be only from him
& will be only his & he will be only mine

A symbol of our love
when I wear his rubies
A symbol
of our love when I wear his rubies
A symbol of our love when I wear
his rubies
it will be because
I will be only his and he will be only mine
when I wear his rubies
when I wear his rubies

# My Yellow Scarf

My yellow scarf

full of perfume

I swiftly & gently pass it through your mouth

& face

I flirt with you

my love

& let the scent linger

you

quickly

grasp me

we remain

within each other

My yellow scarf full of perfume

I flirt with you my love

you quickly

grasp me

as I decorate you as always

full of my chorus & perfume

Arelis Soto

# Heartbeats

Heartbeats within

me

from my heart

sanely

heartbeats

within

me my heart

# Hot Pink

In hot pink

the songbird

is Diastole

and the hummingbird

sometimes, visits

and joins in chorus

the hummingbird likes to peck at the butterfly wherever

it maybe

in chorus

In hot pink

the songbird

is Diastole and when the hummingbird flies

away the red songbird and the bluebird remain as one
breathless or

breathing in love

and what is theirs' is theirs' always

eternally

always was

and remains as such eternally

In hot pink, the songbird is Diastole

the red bird

and the red bird and the blue bird become one as always

a darker shade of purple or any shade of purple

and what is theirs' is theirs' always eternally

always was and remains as such the red bird and the blue bird
two hearts

two

that are one always eternally decorating each other

in-love

always eternally

the songbird is Diastole

the red bird & blue bird become one as always

any shade of purple

white & hot pink any shade always eternally

# Rush Flow

Precious brilliants

placed

set on precious

metals

jewels

& diamonds

send a vivid surprise

to the gift receiver's body

like a blood rush flow

precious

brilliants

placed

set on precious metals

like a blood rush flow

Arelis Soto

# Hand Loyal Play

They hold their hands and twirl their fingers around they play,

with their hands as loyal as they are with each other, they hold
their hands

and twirl their fingers within each other's hands,

they play with their hands in loyal couple's hand


play


and there is nothing else in the world, but just them

involved in their hand play as loyal as they are with each other

They hold their hands and twirl

their fingers within each other's hands

playing with their hands they play with their hands they play

with their hands in a loyal couple's hand play

# I Don't Want

I don't want to live the life of indifference

I shall enjoy the warmthness

of the wind, because

I don't want to live the life of indifference

Arelis Soto

# Orangey Sky

Suttle sky

gentle

atmosphere

I walk by myself

and look up at the orange

Sky

I smell

the perfume

upon my yellow

scarf and my colored

skin

is surrounded by the gentle atmosphere

as I walk by myself

and I look at the orangey sky and this moment

is all mine

# Why Am I

If I'm not in-love
then why am I not distracted from you?
If I'm not in-love then why am I?

* Pink Summersweet

Arelis Soto

# Water

"Cold
water in a cup, glass."

# Somatic

All
everything
somatic
somatic cell
somewhere
unsombered
somebody,
but rather
somehow
specified
known
unsophism
classy
sophisticated
near Somme
drinking wine
writing
soothely
soothely
somewhere unsombered

All

everything

somatic cell

somewhere

unsombered

somebody, but rather somehow someway

specified

known unspoken

classy

Near Somme

accompanied by the solar Sun, soft Sunny day

Summersweet

soft hearted sunrays

sophisticated

whether in solace

or accompanied

somatic cell

somewhere

unsombered and the Solar, Sun, soft Sunny Day

& Winter glow

# Sensation Is Our Sensations

Sensation some kind of love

between you and I

sensation

once and again

sensation

some kind of love

sensation

between you & I

sensations

is our

sensation

in our own definition

sensations

is our sensation

# Me Comprendes

Ahora que me entiendes

me comprendes

mi amor

sabrás

que

siempre

te amo

aunque

yo

este ocupada

en nuestras cosas

sabrás que

siempre

te amo

aunque yo este

ocupada

en nuestras cosas

ahora que me entiendes

me comprendes

mi amor

# I'm Kneeled

Fresh summer air

all around

I'm near

a flower

in my

garden

I'm kneeled down

I caress my

flower

within

my

hands I grasp it

gently

in my garden

summer air

all around

# *Energy*

Full
love energy
between my beloved
and me
full love
energy
Our own
full love
energy
Becomes
&
as the quiet
rain falls against
it's substances

objects

&

so forth

everything becomes settled

&

How

wonderful

the atmosphere becomes

dry,

&

my songbird remains unopressed

# Crimson

His love is a strong heartbeat & crimson

How he involves me, he demonstrates that his love is only for me

He gives me calmness yet, his romance is a strong heartbeat & crimson to me

He involves me

He demonstrates that his love is only for me, he gives me such calmness yet,

His love is a strong heartbeat, with my strong heartbeat, his love seems

Crimson to me as he clearly demonstrates that his love is only for me

# Sweetly & Kindly

You are

everything to me

# Shine

Soaring high

upon

the highest part of

the sky

I saw a distant petite

shine, as I approached it slowly

but surely

that shine

in which

I saw a small petite star

upon the highest

part of the sky

I approached a shine that I held within my hands, grasped that small petite

shine

Soaring togetherly and I held that shine within my hands

Togetherly & within the sky that shine which is my star

and many stars shine high upon the highest

part of the sky

I approach it

It is my star and many stars all around

Shining, high upon the highest part of the elegant

Nocturnal dark sky

Soaring surely togetherly

within my hands

Arelis Soto

# Remain Or Flies

My songbird

remains or flies

freely

In the sky

or earthly

remains

or flies

freely

# Caress & Hold

I pass a feather upon

his cheek to wake him gently

We

caress & hold

each other

immensely

& begin to kiss

over & once more, we

caress & hold

each other

immensely

I passed a feather upon his cheek

Arelis Soto

# *Innocently, Actually*

To foolishly love the fool in love with you
For loving each other this way


is


Unfoolishly
& actually true love
innocently
We are in love

# Every night

A stable star
I find every night
and it shines for me
it shines
every night
a stable star

Arelis Soto

# Nature All Around Me

The cool breeze

gentle upon me

around

softly

naturally

nature

all around me

gentle upon me,

the cool breeze

I am grateful

# Already Kissed

If foolishly you shall feel deceived, it must be when thow
believes that thow's kisses

are not my truest, for when I first will kiss will be, with only
you

& do not suppose, but know this is

true

for a kiss is not a kiss

where love cannot be found true

for in pursuit to future

one can remember

a fallacy

& then perceive

correctly & know,

but not suppose

that a kiss is not a kiss

where love cannot be found

true,

for If foolishly

you shall feel deceived it must be when

thow believes that

thow's kisses are not my truest

for when I first kiss, it will

be with only you, there my kisses will remain only with you

and if for now, we are in our waiting, let our wait not be for
too long

we have already waited for when I first kiss,

will be with only you,

there my kisses will remain, only with you

there our kisses will remain

just me just you

for a kiss is truly a kiss is truly a kiss only where true love

can be found true

for my first true kiss

will be found & will remain with you, their our kisses will
remain

just me & just you

there will be no-one else & no foolishness

shall make you feel deceived

any longer for our kisses will be stronger

than a Citadel, but beautiful like a Private Paradise

for a kiss, where love can be found true for my first true kiss

will be found and will remain just me and just you

beautiful like a Private Paradise for a kiss is truly an unfoolish

kiss, where love can be found true

for my first true kiss will be found and will remain with only
you there our kisses

will remain just me and just you a Private Paradise

there I shall have no complain with the true kiss

Arelis Soto

# Passion, Sweating, Smoothe

Watch me

Watch you

person to person

face to face

love from me

love from you

just too good

we're mouth to mouth

kissing

love smoothe

sensitive

passion, sweating, smoothe

watch me, watch you

person to person

face to face

love from me

love from you

# Already Kissed

There will be no-one else

& no foolishness

shall make you feel

deceived

*Personal records only
*Love in our own loyal definition

Arelis Soto

# *Setting*

A secret

setting

for my

beloved

& I

unknown to us ourselves

at first

&

then

revealed

& such a wonderful

surprise

secret setting

for my beloved

& I

# *Flower Flutters*

A

gentle flower flutters it's

petals in bloom

and caresses

grazes

the skin

it touches

or like a beak, butterfly

or bee that flies by

unharmfully

a gentle flower flutters

Arelis Soto

# Always Find Each Other

Swoosh

Swoosh

red bird

blue bird

ourselves

we always find each other

swoosh

swoosh red & blue bird

become purple

ourselves

you & I

always find each

other

# Reír

Reír

gozar

reír

feliz

reír

gozar

somos

feliz

reír

y

gozar

somos feliz

# Soplando

Soplando

notas

cuando

quiero

soplando

notas

pajaritos, pajarones

y voy soplando

notas

cuando quiero

soplando notas

# Happiness

Music

that

brings

happiness

only

happiness

expressively

lively

eternally happily

music

that

brings

happiness

only

happiness

expressively

lively

eternally

happily

music

# *Kaleidoscope*

Cluster of colours

unpatterned to

pertain toith the

artistic expression of

the Kaleidoscope

turning

triangle

sets

cluster of colours

# Yellow Arch

Clear

yellow arch

striped

within

the clear

& now

clear

yellow arch

striped

within

the

clear & now

Arelis Soto

# By The Sea

Out of the water

onto the sand

the breeze passes us by

whirling

around us

by the sea

on the beach, the sand

& you put your head on my head

we rub heads gently

& you linger in my

hair locks

out of the sand

the breeze around

us, you & me, by the sea

we rub heads

gently & you linger

in my hair locks

# Solos

La arena

abrigarte

miradas

entre tú y yo

hablamos cosas

fieles

amorosas

la noche

oscura

nos llenamos

de besos

y todo amoroso

hablamos

entre tú y yo

nosotros solos

nuestras miradas

están, puestas

entre tú y yo

mirándonos

nuestras bocas se

silencian con

nuestros besos
entre tú y yo
cada paso
dice algo
fiel,
nuestras bocas se
silencian
bocas fieles
amorosas
la noche oscura
nos llenamos de besos
nosotros solos fieles

con bocas amorosas

vivos

nuestra locura sana

hablamos con nuestras

bocas de silencio

bocas fieles

amorosas, enamoradas

nuestra bocas se

silencian

La arena abrigarte

estamos solos

enamorados

Arelis Soto

# Opal Butterfly

Opal teared

white & glittered

only mine

uncompared Opal

teared white &

glittered

vindicated Emeralds

& rubies

only mine

uncompared

with gladioluses

all around

it

# We Remain

We remain
away inside
ourselves
you dry my tears


safely you keep me


only you & I


We remain away
inside
ourselves
no doubts
you & I
we remain
safely inside
you dry my
tears
in the darkness
you & I, we are as
always one

Arelis Soto

# Real Control

Real control

is

calm

serenity

relaxing

smoothly


real control

is calm


serenely

relaxing, smoothly

undecadent

# Siempre

abre nuestra puerta

esta abierta somos dos amantes eres tu

soy yo

como siempre

envueltos

en nuestro

amor

por nuestras

palabras

de nosotros

recordando

nuestras palabras siempre llegan

siempre estas

abre nuestra puerta

esta abierta

Somos dos amantes

tu y yo nada mas

# Preciously

Although I love you
let this love fly
free
fly free
preciously
Although I love you
& you love me
let this love fly free

# In A Garden

In a garden with many flowers within a trellis

here or there

kittens & puppies

are there at times

walnuts can gather

for natures' little

animals, for

them to eat

a bench here or there with swings

around too

fuchsia

roses wildly pink

& all flower's

in variation so

blatantly suttle

in gathered

arrangement

In a garden with

many flowers

Arelis Soto

# Every

Every bird flies
Every bird soars
high in flight
takes an air flight
curve
in flight
Every bird soars
Every bird flies
high into the sky
by day
by night
Every bird flies
Every bird soars
high in the true
blue sky
or skimming low
into the
variable green
waters

just enough
to shimmer some
water on their
flocked feathers
Every bird flies
Every bird soars
Every bird must
fly
Every bird must
soar
Every bird flies
Every bird soars

# When

When
you kiss me
I get dizzy
in an invisible
atmosphere of love
I feel
all of your
love for me
oooo! all of you
love
when you kiss me
my love

# *Sour Cucumbers*

Cucumbers, vinegar,

water, salt,

vinegar flavors

all natural

ingredients

# Periwinkle

Walk into my

house

& there

is a doggy

winking

at me

walk into

my

house

and there is

a doggy

winking at me

# Flores En Plentitude

Flores refrescante

muchos besos

de tu amor

flores refrescante

flores en multitude

muchos besos

acaricias

de tu amor

flores refrescante

muchos besos

de tu amor

flores en plentitude

# *Lovable*

There was thee time
thee moment
deep inside
perceptionally
introverted
deep inside
There was thee time
thee moment
forever
perceptionally
introverted
deep inside
fluttering
forever
forever
fluttering
in-love
forever
felt

deep inside

there was thee

time

thee moment

perceptionally

introverted

deep inside

thy's

love

is felt

deep inside

fluttering

in-love

forever

there was thee time

thee moment

that love is more

than a day dream

# *Lovable*

more than a secret fantasy

settled

yet fluttering

deep inside

perceptive

deep inside

introverted

spoken

"I love the smell of you have as when it is fluttered is relinquished into calmness from it"

in-love

forever

there is thee time

thee moment

that love-is more

than a daydream

more than a secret fantasy

there was a time

thee moment

perceptionally

introverted

deep inside

thy's love

is felt deep

inside

fluttering

in love

forever

bliss

Arelis Soto

# Something In My Heart

Something in my heart
It was Saturday night

It was demonstrated clearly
it was Saturday

Something in my heart
Your all the love
that I own
Our couple's love
you wanted me to feel
your love that you have for me
It was Saturday night
you sang to me

You needed me
something in of my heart
It was demonstrated
clearly

Your all the love that

I own

You needed that

It was demonstrated

clearly & you got it that I got you, my love


It was Saturday night

that has developed into everyday,

ooh! ever so eternal

ever so you

ever so me

It was Saturday night

. . . into ever so eternal

ever so you, ever so me

that is everyday

# Donde Aye

Donde hay

el amor real y veraz

estará la piedad que

es también real y veraz

muchas veces vemos los ayes de la vida

y sus variedades aspectuales

pero siempre donde hay el amor

real y veraz

estará la piedad

que es real y veraz

# The Awaiting

Time passes
love endures


&

has no measure

for

the truest

of

Love in all

of it's

Realism


in

life & thereafter

Arelis Soto

# Sound And Resound

When we are

near each

other, our

emotions alter from you

to me, from me to you

the

heartbeat

our

heartbeats sound

& resound & we

only hear our heartbeats

when we are near each

other, our emotions alter

It might be shy, it might

be joyful, from you to me

the

heartbeat

our heartbeats sound &

resound & we only

hear our

heartbeats

When we are near

each other our emotions

alter, just

you & I

Arelis Soto

# Place

In the most

secretive

cloud

In the most happiest

place

there will

await

for you my love

In the most happiest

place

there I will gaze upon

your eyes

as we meet

face

to face

my love

# *Expressions*

Expressions

of love

many facets

vindicates quietly

our loyal love for each other, thy's love for one another

expressions of love literally

Arelis Soto

# *Many Forms*

Thee many forms

of holding

each

other's hands

literally

# *My life*

I am a mother.

I have never experienced being in love with anyone.

I have worked in different places with archived documents of my educational work etc . . .

I have strong beliefs' in love.

All my life I was busy working.

I am grateful for my strong beliefs' of love.

I thought I would write my thoughts of love & make it into a book.

I have worked for Private Educational Institutions for Higher learning.

Truly,

Arelis Soto